5-Step Handicrafts for Kids

Christmas

Anna Llimós

4880 Lower Valley Road, Atglen, PA 19310

Christmas

Copyright © 2021 by Schiffer Publishing, Ltd.

Originally published as *Navidad* by Anna Llimós
© Parramón Paidotribo S.L. - Spain
Translated from the Spanish by Ian Hayden Jones

Library of Congress Control Number: 2020952756

All rights reserved. No part of this work may be reproduced or used in any form or by any means—graphic, electronic, or mechanical, including photocopying or information storage and retrieval systems—without written permission from the publisher.

The scanning, uploading, and distribution of this book or any part thereof via the Internet or any other means without the permission of the publisher is illegal and punishable by law. Please purchase only authorized editions and do not participate in or encourage the electronic piracy of copyrighted materials.

"Schiffer Kids" logo is a trademark of Schiffer Publishing, Ltd.
Amelia logo is a trademark of Schiffer Publishing, Ltd.
Type set in Fink/Avenir/Windsor

ISBN: 978-0-7643-6215-6
Printed in China

Published by Schiffer Kids
An imprint of Schiffer Publishing, Ltd.
4880 Lower Valley Road
Atglen, PA 19310
Phone: (610) 593-1777; Fax: (610) 593-2002
E-mail: Info@schifferbooks.com
Web: www.schifferbooks.com

For our complete selection of fine books on this and related subjects, please visit our website at www.schifferbooks.com. You may also write for a free catalog.

Schiffer Publishing's titles are available at special discounts for bulk purchases for sales promotions or premiums. Special editions, including personalized covers, corporate imprints, and excerpts, can be created in large quantities for special needs. For more information, contact the publisher.

We are always looking for people to write books on new and related subjects. If you have an idea for a book, please contact us at proposals@schifferbooks.com.

Other Schiffer Books in the Series:

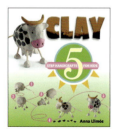

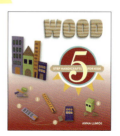
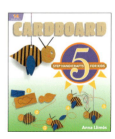
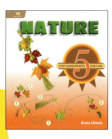

Contents

PLACE CARD CLIPS
P. 4

LITTLE ANGEL
P. 6

CHRISTMAS BALLS
P. 8

HOLIDAY CARDS
P. 10

WRAPPING PAPER
P. 12

REINDEER AND SLEIGH
P. 14

GIFT TAGS
P. 16

SANTA CARD HOLDER
P. 18

CHRISTMAS TREE
P. 20

GARLAND
P. 22

HOLIDAY FLOWER FRIEND
P. 24

WINTER WONDERLAND SCENE
P. 26

JINGLE BELLS
P. 28

CHRISTMAS STAR
P. 30

Place card clips

MATERIALS

Orange, red, green, brown, pink, and black putty or clay
Orange, red, and green cardstock
Red, green, yellow, and white paints
Clothespins
A gimlet or an awl
White glue
Latex varnish
Scissors
A paintbrush

1 Paint one clothespin red, another yellow, and a third green. Once they are dry, decorate them with white polka dots.

2 Roll up two small clay balls, one red and the other orange, and glue them together. Make some green clay leaves and score on some veins with your gimlet.

3 Make a tiny tree by gluing a green clay cone to a brown clay cylinder. Use your gimlet to add some detail.

4 Make the parts of Santa's head shown in the picture and join them together.

5 Cut three different-colored cards and glue your figurines on top of the clothespins. A coat of latex varnish will help protect them.

Add names so that everyone knows where to sit for Christmas dinner!

Little angel

MATERIALS

Cardboard toilet paper roll
Blue, green, pink, and black paints
Yellow felt
Cotton
A black felt-tip pen
White glue
Scissors
A paintbrush

1 Draw the shape of your angel on the cardboard toilet paper roll (the head and body on one side, the wings on the other).

2 Carefully cut along the lines you have drawn.

3 Paint her body green and face pink.

4 Paint her wings and the stripes on her dress in blue.

5 Cut and shape the yellow felt then glue it to her head to make hair, before painting on black eyes, a mouth, and a nose.

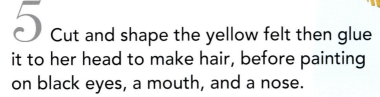

A lovely angel floats on a cloud.

Christmas balls

MATERIALS

Foam spheres
Blue, purple, and pink tissue papers
Natural and green raffia ribbons
Purple putty or clay
Paper clips
Latex varnish
A paintbrush
Scissors

1 Cut lots of small squares of blue, purple, and pink tissue paper.

2 Stick them to the polystyrene spheres with latex varnish.

3 Form a small purple clay cone and use the latex varnish again to attach it to the sphere.

4 Push a paper clip into the clay.

5 Thread two pieces of raffia (one natural and one green) and tie them off.

Decorate your Christmas tree!

Holiday cards

MATERIALS

Yellow and orange cardstock
Brown and blue corrugated cardboard
White glue
Scissors

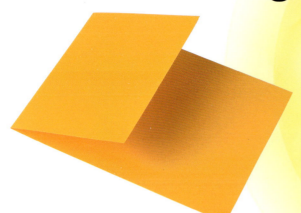

1 Cut out a rectangle of yellow cardstock and fold it as shown.

2 Stick a rectangle of orange cardstock inside.

3 Draw two stars on the back of your blue and brown corrugated cardboard. Cut them out.

4 Glue the blue star to the top-left front corner of your card.

5 Glue the brown star in the center, so that half of it overlaps the orange cardstock underneath. The possibilities are endless!

Wish all of your friends Seasons Greetings!

11

Wrapping paper

MATERIALS

A sheet of polystyrene
Cork bottle stoppers
Plain blue wrapping paper
Orange, green, and red paints
A black permanent marker
White glue
Scissors
A paintbrush
A pencil

1 Cut a square from the polystyrene sheet and draw a star shape in permanent marker. Then make grooves along your lines by scoring out some of the polystyrene with the tip of your pencil.

2 Glue a cork bottle stopper to the back of the polystyrene sheet.

3 Dip it in orange paint.

12

4 Press your stamp onto the wrapping paper, so that the impression of the star can be clearly seen.

5 Cover the paper in stars. Create different impressions, then try combining the shapes for more possibilities.

Personalize your gifts!

Reindeer and sleigh

MATERIALS

Brown cardstock
Dark-brown cardstock
Red corrugated cardboard
Two clothespins
A black felt-tip pen
Orange and brown colored pencils
Thick green and red threads
A glue stick
Scissors

1 Draw and cut out the shapes of your reindeer's head and horns.

2 Glue the horns on top of its head and draw on a face.

3 Clip on the legs (clothespins) and affix two small pieces of dark-brown cardstock as hooves.

4 Draw and cut out the sides and floor of the sleigh.

5 Glue the sleigh together and then bridle your reindeer to it with the thick green and red threads.

... all ready to give Santa a helping hand!

Gift tags

MATERIALS

Air-dry clay
Orange, red, green, blue, yellow, and white paints
A rolling pin
A toothbrush
A plastic knife
Colored ribbons
A gimlet or an awl
A paintbrush

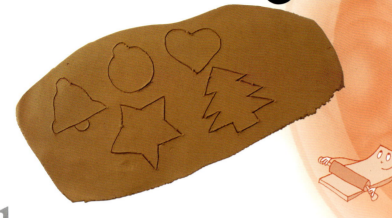

1. Use the rolling pin to make a flat sheet of air-dry clay and use your gimlet to score out the shapes of a Christmas tree, a bell, a ball, a star, and a heart.

2. Cut out the clay shapes with your plastic knife.

3. With a gimlet, punch small holes at the top of each shape.

4 Once the clay has dried, paint the shapes in different colors.

5 Paint some patterns onto your shapes; you can even create a snowy effect with a toothbrush. Thread different-colored ribbons through the holes that you made.

Making your presents even more special!

Santa card holder

MATERIALS

Red, white, black, and pink felts
Clothespins
Yellow and green paints
Cotton
A paintbrush
White glue
Scissors

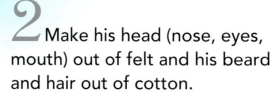

1 Cut off a long, narrow strip of red felt to make Santa's body and two black felt boots the same width.

2 Make his head (nose, eyes, mouth) out of felt and his beard and hair out of cotton.

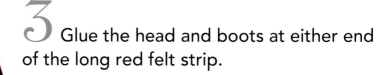

3 Glue the head and boots at either end of the long red felt strip.

4 Make Santa's hat out of felt and stick it onto his head.

5 Paint two clothespins green and two yellow. Clip them to your card holder once they are dry.

Showcase all of your Christmas cards!

Christmas tree

1 Draw and cut out two tree shapes from green cardstock. Make a cut in one of them from the top to the center and in the other from the bottom to the center.

MATERIALS

Orange, yellow, and red felts
Green cardstock
Laminated corkboard
White glue
Scissors
A pencil

2 Slot the two pieces together.

3 Glue eight pieces of laminated cork board around the base of your tree to make the trunk.

4 Cut out circles of red, yellow, and orange felt and stick them all over your tree's branches.

5 Tie off an orange felt bow and stick it to the top of your tree.

Isn't it lovely!

Garland

MATERIALS

Orange and red cardstock
Green and orange raffia ribbon
White glue
Scissors
A ruler
A pencil

1 Cut two long, narrow strips of red and orange cardstock and glue them together at a right angle.

2 Start to make your first star by folding the strips successively one over the other.

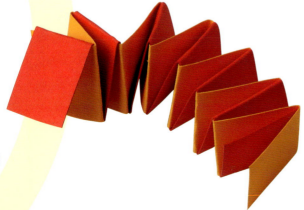

3 Keep folding until you get to the end of the strips.

4 Glue the ends of the strips together. You can make different-colored stars.

5 Cut off two strands of raffia ribbon and pass them through the center of your stars.

Holiday-inspired garlands.

Holiday flower friend

MATERIALS

Light-brown, red, and green cardstock
White cardstock
Natural raffia ribbon
Red, green, and white colored pencils
A black felt-tip pen
A long, thin wooden stick
A glue stick
Adhesive tape
Scissors

1 Draw and cut out your friend's dress and hat sections in red and white cardstock, then glue them together.

2 Cut out two green legs and decorate them with red stripes. Add green and white stripes to the hat and dress.

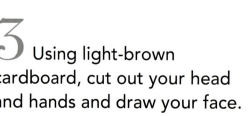

3 Using light-brown cardboard, cut out your head and hands and draw your face.

4 Glue the different parts together, sticking a few strands of raffia ribbon underneath her hat for hair.

5 Affix the wooden stick to her back with a little adhesive tape.

Add a bit of extra cheer to Christmas flowers.

25

Winter wonderland scene

MATERIALS

Brown, green, and yellow cardstock
Red corrugated cardboard
White, orange, red, green, purple, and black putty or clay
A plastic spatula
A glue stick
Scissors
Latex varnish
A paintbrush

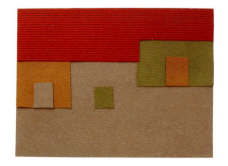

1 Cut out the shapes of houses and doors from different-colored cardstock and stick them onto a background of brown cardstock.

2 Cut out and glue on a red corrugated cardboard rooftop.

3 Cover the ground with white clay and scoop out the paths with a spatula.

4. Make a snowman by sticking two circles of white clay onto your picture. Use small balls of black clay for the eyes. Glue small balls of clay all over the scene for snowflakes.

5. Make him an orange clay nose, then his hat, scarf, and buttons. Paint on a layer of varnish once you have finished.

Hang it on the wall in your bedroom!

Jingle bells

MATERIALS

A cardboard egg carton
Red, green, orange, and white paints
A length of red ribbon
A toothbrush
Small round (jingle!) bells
A gimlet or an awl
A paintbrush

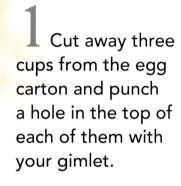

1 Cut away three cups from the egg carton and punch a hole in the top of each of them with your gimlet.

2 Paint one of them red, another orange, and the last one green.

3 Decorate them with stripes and use the toothbrush to create a snowy effect with white paint.

4 Tie a round bell to the end of the red ribbon and then pass the ribbon through the hole at the top of one of your egg cups.

5 Tie on another bell a bit farther up the ribbon and thread on another cup. Repeat this process with the last bell and cup.

Jingling all the way to Christmas Day!

Christmas star

MATERIALS

Yellow cardstock
Red, orange, pink, brown, and blue colored pencils
Yellow string
A black felt-tip pen
A glue stick
White paper
Scissors

1. Draw and cut out the pictured star and tail shapes from yellow cardstock.

2. Draw a face onto the star with your black felt-tip pen and glue it to the tail. Attach a length of colored string, so you can hang it up later.

3. Draw and cut out the pictured figure from white paper.

4 Color the figure with your pencils and fold its hands forward.

5 Draw and cut out a white paper hat, then color it red before gluing it to the star. Hang the figure from the tail by its hands.

Follow that star!

Christmas

Can I do it?

- These fourteen models are super-easy to make; however, some are simpler than others. Check the table below so that you can decide which objects are best suited to you. But you can definitely make them all!

- If any of the modeling stages prove difficult or complicated, you can always ask an adult for help.

What will I need?

- The materials used to create these handicrafts are easy to find at home. Just remember to save all of the packaging and wrapping items that you would otherwise throw away or recycle!

- If you don't find exactly what you need, just use your imagination and substitute it for something similar!

Is there anything else I should know?

- Varnishing your putty or clay handicrafts will make them longer-lasting and easier to clean. We recommend that you apply latex varnish with a paintbrush.

- While all of the materials used for these handicrafts are easy to cut with scissors or pierce with a gimlet, you should always ask an adult for help!

SOME ARE EASIER THAN OTHERS

★

- Christmas balls
- Holiday cards
- Garland
- Christmas star

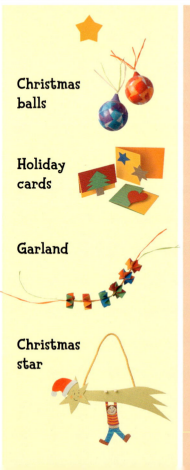

★★

- Place card clips
- Wrapping paper
- Gift tags
- Holiday flower friend
- Jingle bells

★★★

- Little angel
- Santa card holder
- Winter wonderland scene

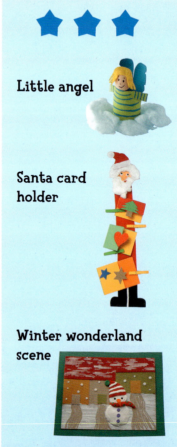

★★★★

- Reindeer and sleigh
- Christmas tree